THE *ANGELUS* AND *REGINA CAELI*
IN LATIN AND ENGLISH

THE *ANGELUS* AND *REGINA CAELI*
IN LATIN AND ENGLISH

Edited by
Geoffrey W.M.P. Lopes da Silva

DOMINA NOSTRA PUBLISHING
Monterey, California, USA

Published in 2021 by
Domina Nostra Publishing, Inc.
P.O. Box 1464, Monterey, CA. 93942-1464 USA
Email: info@DominaNostraPublishing.com
Website: www.DominaNostraPublishing.com

Copyright © 2021 Domina Nostra Publishing, Inc.

Printed and bound in the United States.
All rights reserved.

Although the editor and publisher have made every effort to ensure the accuracy and completeness of information contained in this book, we assume no responsibility for errors, inaccuracies, omissions, or any inconsistency herein. Any slights of people, places, or organizations are unintentional, and will be corrected in the next edition.

ISBN: 978-0-9741900-6-8

First printing, 2021

"The value of contemplation on the mystery of the Incarnation of the Word, of the greeting to the Virgin, and of recourse to her merciful intercession remains unchanged".

Saint Paul VI
Marialis Cultus, n. 41

«*Cum integra vis contemplationis, quæ in mysterium Incarnationis Verbi fertur, salutationis angelicæ Virgini impertitæ significatio, imploratio miserentis eius intercessionis immutatæ maneant*».

Sanctus Paulus VI
Marialis Cultus, n. 41

Introduction

The *Angelus* is a Marian prayer devotion in honour of the Incarnation of the Lord. The *Angelus* consists of three versicles with their responses, each followed by a Hail Mary, and concluding with a brief verse with its response and one of two prayers from *The Roman Missal* (*Missale Romanum*).

Traditionally, the *Angelus* is prayed in the morning, at midday, and in the evening, marked by the ringing of the *angelus*-bell. The ringing of the *angelus*-bell consists of three strokes followed by a pause three times, and then nine strokes, usually at 6am, noon, and 6pm. The *Angelus* is traditionally said standing on Saturdays and Sundays (genuflecting at the third versicle) but kneeling at other times.

In his 1974 apostolic exhortation *Marialis cultus*, Pope St Paul VI said:

> What we have to say about the *Angelus Domini* is meant to be only a simple but earnest exhortation to continue its traditional recitation wherever and whenever possible. The *Angelus Domini* does not need to be revised, because of its simple structure, its biblical character, its historical origin which links it to the prayer for peace and safety, and its quasi-liturgical rhythm which sanctifies different moments during the day, and because it reminds us of the Paschal Mystery, in which recalling the Incarnation of the Son of God we pray that we may "by His Passion and Cross be brought to the glory of His Resurrection" (*The Roman Missal*, Fourth Sunday of Advent, *Collect*. Similarly the *Collect* of 25 March, which may be used in place of the previous one in the recitation of the *Angelus Domini*).

These factors ensure that the *Angelus Domini* despite the passing of centuries retains an unaltered value and an intact freshness. It is true that certain customs traditionally linked with the recitation of the *Angelus Domini* have disappeared or can continue only with difficulty in modern life. But these are marginal elements. The value of contemplation on the mystery of the Incarnation of the Word, of the greeting to the Virgin, and of recourse to her merciful intercession remains unchanged. And despite the changed conditions of the times, for the majority of people there remain unaltered the characteristic periods of the day—morning, noon and evening—which mark the periods of their activity and constitute an invitation to pause in prayer.[1]

---

[1] Sermo hic Noster de prece *Angelus Domini* ad id tantum spectat, ut Nostram adhortationem iteremus, simplicem sed ardentem, ut huiusmodi orationis consueta recitatio, quantum fieri possit, servetur. Nec videtur eadem oratio esse instauranda; post tot enim sæculorum decursum eius continuatur vis et nitor, siquidem eius structura simplex est atque de divinis Litteris deprompta; origo eius historica ad invocationem revocat, qua incolumitas in pace expetitur; liturgicus præterea eius cursus certa diei tempora quodammodo consecrat; ad paschale denique mysterium commemorandum inducit; nam cognita Filii Dei Incarnatione, petimus, ut «*per passionem eius et crucem ad resurrectionis gloriam perducamur*» (*Missale Romanum*, Dominica IV Adventus, *Collecta*. Simile quiddam in *Collecta* diei 25 Martii continetur, quæ in recitanda precatione *Angelus Domini* pro priore, in textu propositi, substitui potest).

Re quidem vera nonnullæ consuetudines, quæ e tradito more recitationem orationis *Angelus Domini* comitabantur, iam ablata sunt, aut vix in hodierna hominum vita animadvertuntur; de rebus tamen parvi momenti agitur, cum integra vis contemplationis, quæ in mysterium Incarnationis Verbi fertur, salutationis angelicæ Virgini impertitæ significatio, imploratio miserentis eius intercessions immutatæ maneant. Quamvis præterea mutatæ sint temporum condiciones, eadem semper pro plerisque hominibus perstant certa quædam diei tempora, mane, meridies et vesper, utpote quæ operum eorum vices significent simulque ad quandam precationis causa moram interponendam moneant (SANCTUS PAULUS VI, Adhortatio Apostolica *Marialis cultus* (2 februarii 1974), n. 41: *Acta Apostolicae Sedis* 66 (1974), pp. 113-168.

Introduction

During Easter Time (*tempus paschale*), the *Angelus* is replaced with the *Regina cæli*. This prayer consists of the Marian antiphon (*antiphona mariana*), which are the first two versicles with their responses, followed by a concluding versicle and response, and an Easter collect prayer from the *Missale Romanum* (Roman Missal). The *Regina cæli* is said standing.

Dating back to the 12th century, the authorship of the *Regina cæli* is unknown, though it has been ascribed without good reason to Pope Gregory V (c. 972-999). Legend says that Saint Gregory I, the Great (c. 540-604) heard the first three lines chanted by angels on a certain Easter morning in Rome while he walked barefoot in a great religious procession and that the saint thereupon added the fourth line: *ora pro nobis Deum, allelúia.*

Continuing a custom that began in the pontificate of Pope St John XXIII (1881-1963), His Holiness the Pope gives an address every Sunday at noon, at the end of which the *Angelus* or *Regina cæli* is prayed, before giving his apostolic blessing (*benedictio apostolica*). This address is broadcast throughout the world. Due to this connection with the *Angelus* and *Regina cæli* to the Most Holy Father, the Prayer for the Pope (*Oratio pro papa*) has been included for recitation following the *Angelus* or *Regina caeli*.

A custom originating in Italy adds the Minor Doxology (*doxologia minor*) or Glory to the Father (*Gloria Patri*) three times to the *Angelus* in thanksgiving to the Blessed Trinity for the privileges bestowed upon the Blessed Virgin Mary. Another custom originating in Italy is the reciting of the *De profundis* (Psalm 129 [130]) for the faithful departed immediately after the evening recitation of the *Angelus*.

Angelus Domini et Regina cæli

PER ANNUM

℣. Angelus Dómini nuntiávit Maríæ.

℟. Et concépit de Spíritu Sancto.

℣. Ave, María, grátia plena, Dóminus tecum:
benedícta tu in muliéribus,
et benedíctus fructus ventris tui, Iesus.

(*Lc* 1, 28. 42)

℟. Sancta María, Mater Dei,
ora pro nobis peccatóribus,
nunc et in hora mortis nostræ. Amen.

℣. Ecce ancílla Dómini.

℟. Fiat mihi secúndum verbum tuum.

(*Lc* 1, 38)

℣. Ave, María… ℟. Sancta María…

℣. *Et Verbum caro factum est.*

℟. *Et habitávit in nobis.*

(*Io* 1, 14)

℣. Ave, María… ℟. Sancta María…

℣. Ora pro nobis, Sancta Dei Génetrix.

℟. Ut digni efficiámur
promissionibus Christi.

Orémus.

The *Angelus* and the *Regina cæli*

THROUGHOUT THE YEAR

℣. THE ANGEL OF THE LORD declared unto Mary.

℟. And she conceived by the Holy Spirit.

℣. Hail, Mary, full of grace, the Lord is with thee: blessed art thou among women, and blessed is the fruit of thy womb, Jesus.
(*Luke* 1:28, 42)

℟. Holy Mary, Mother of God, pray for us sinners, now and at the hour of our death. Amen.

℣. Behold the handmaid of the Lord.

℟. Be it done unto me according to Your word.
(*Luke* 1:38)

℣. Hail, Mary… ℟. Holy Mary…

℣. *And the Word was made flesh.*

℟. *And dwelt among us.*
(*John* 1:14)

℣. Hail, Mary… ℟. Holy Mary…

℣. Pray for us, O holy Mother of God.

℟. That we may be made worthy of the promises of Christ.

Let us pray.

Grátiam tuam, quæsumus, Dómine,
méntibus nostris infúnde,
ut qui, ángelo nuntiánte,
Christi Fílii tui incarnatiónem cognóvimus,
per passiónem eius et crucem
ad resurrectiónis glóriam perducámur.
Per eúndem Christum Dóminum nostrum. ℟. Amen.

Vel:

Deus,
qui Verbum tuum in útero Vírginis Maríæ
veritátem carnis humánæ suscípere voluísti,
concéde, quæsumus, ut,
qui Redemptórem nostrum Deum
et hóminem confitémur,
ipsíus étiam divínæ natúræ mereámur esse consórtes.
Per Christum Dóminum nostrum. ℟. Amen.

The Angelus

Pour forth, we beseech You, O Lord,
Your grace into our hearts,
that we, to whom the Incarnation of Christ Your Son
was made known by the message of an Angel,
may, by his Passion and Cross
be brought to the glory of his Resurrection.
Through the same Christ our Lord. ℟. Amen.

Or:

O God,
who willed that your Word should take on the reality
of human flesh in the womb of the Virgin Mary,
grant, we pray, that we,
who confess our Redeemer to be God and man,
may merit to become partakers
even in his divine nature.
Through the same Christ our Lord. ℟. Amen.

TEMPUS PASCHALE

℣. Regína cæli, lætáre, allelúia.

℟. Quia quem meruísti portáre, allelúia.

℣. Resurréxit, sicut dixit, allelúia.

℟. Ora pro nobis Deum, allelúia.

℣. Gaude et lætáre, Virgo María, allelúia.

℟. Quia surréxit Dóminus vere, allelúia.

Orémus.

Deus,
qui per resurrectiónem Fílii tui,
Dómini nostri Iesu Christi,
mundum lætificáre dignátus es: præsta, quǽsumus;
ut, per eius Genetrícem Vírginem Maríam,
perpétuæ capiámus gáudia vitæ.
Per eúndem Christum Dóminum nostrum. ℟. Amen.

EASTER TIME

℣. QUEEN OF HEAVEN, rejoice, alleluia!

℟. For He whom you did merit to bear, alleluia!

℣. Has risen, as He said, alleluia!

℟. Pray for us to God, alleluia!

℣. Rejoice and be glad, O Virgin Mary, alleluia!

℟. For the Lord is truly risen, alleluia.

Let us pray.

O God,
who have been pleased to gladden the world
by the Resurrection of your Son our Lord Jesus Christ,
grant, we pray,
that through his Mother, the Virgin Mary,
we may receive the joys of everlasting life.
Through the same Christ our Lord. ℟. Amen.

CONCLUSIO

Ters:

℣. Glória Patri, et Fílio,
et Spirítui Sancto.

℟. Sicut erat in princípio, et nunc et semper,
et in saécula sæculórum. Amen.

℣. Pro fidélibus defúnctis:
Réquiem ætérnam dona eis, Dómine.

℟. Et lux perpétua lúceat eis.

℣. Requiéscant in pace.

℟. Amen.

CONCLUSION

Three times:

℣. Glory to the Father, and to the Son,
   and to the Holy Spirit.

℟. As it was in the beginning, is now,
   and will be for ever. Amen.[1]

℣. For the faithful departed:
   Eternal rest grant unto them, O Lord.

℟. And let perpetual light shine upon them.

℣. May they rest in peace.

℟. Amen.

---

[1] Alternate Translation:

Glory be to the Father, and to the Son,
and to the Holy Spirit.
As it was in the beginning, is now
and ever shall be, world without end. Amen.

Oratio pro Papa

℣. Orémus pro Pontífice nostro N.

℟. Dóminus consérvet eum, et vivíficet eum,
et beátum fáciat eum in terra,
et non tradat eum in ánimam inimicórum eius.

(Psalmus 40 [41], 3)

℣. Fiat manus tuas super virum déxteræ tuæ.

℟. Et super fílium tuum quia confirmásti tibi.

Orémus.

Deus,
ómnium fidélium pastor et rector, fámulum tuum N.,
quem pastórem Ecclésiæ tuæ præésse voluísti,
propítius réspice;
da ei, quǽsumus,
verbo et exémplo, quibus præest profícere,
ut ad vitam, una cum grege sibi crédito,
pervéniat sempitérnam.
Per Christum Dóminum nostrum. ℟. Amen.

Conclusion

PRAYER FOR THE POPE

℣. Let us pray for our Pontiff N.

℟. May the Lord preserve him, and give him life,
and bless him upon earth,
and deliver him not to the will of his enemies.
(Psalm 40 [41], 3)

℣. May Your hand be upon Your holy servant.

℟. And upon Your son whom You have anointed.

Let us pray.

O God,
shepherd and ruler of all the faithful,
look favourably on Your servant N.,
whom You have set at the head of Your Church
as her shepherd;
grant, we pray, that by word and example
he may be of service to those over whom he presides
so that, together with the flock entrusted to his care,
he may come to everlasting life.
Through Christ our Lord. ℟. Amen.

Psalmus 129 (130)

¹De profúndis clamávi ad te, Dómine;
²Dómine, exáudi vocem meam.
Fiant aures tuæ intendéntes
in vocem deprecatiónis meæ.

³Si iniquitátes observáveris, Dómine,
Dómine, quis sustinébit?
⁴Quia apud te propitiátio est,
ut timeámus te.

⁵Sustínui te, Dómine,
sustínuit ánima mea in verbo eius;
sperávit ⁶ ánima mea in Dómino
magis quam custódes auróram.

Magis quam custódes auróram
⁷speret Israel in Dómino,
quia apud Dóminum misericórdia,
et copiósa apud eum redémptio.
⁸Et ipse rédimet Israel
ex ómnibus iniquitátibus eius.

℣. Réquiem ætérnam dona eis, Dómine.
℟. Et lux perpétua lúceat eis.

℣. Requiéscant in pace.
℟. Amen.

Orémus.

Deus, véniæ largítor
et humánæ salútis amátor,
quǽsumus cleméntiam tuam, ut
nostræ congregatiónis fratres,
propínquos et benefactóres,
qui ex hoc sǽculo transiérunt,
beáta María semper Vírgine intercedénte
cum ómnibus Sanctis tuis,
ad perpétuæ beatitúdinis
consórtium perveníre concédas.
Per Christum Dóminum nostrum. ℟. Amen.

PSALM 129 (130)

¹OUT OF THE DEPTHS I cry to you, O LORD;
²Lord, hear my voice!
O let your ears be attentive
to the sound of my pleadings.

³If you, O LORD, should mark iniquities,
Lord, who could stand?
⁴But with you is found forgiveness,
that you may be revered.

⁵I long for you, O LORD,
my soul longs for his word.
⁶My soul awaits the Lord
more than watchmen for daybreak.

More than watchmen for daybreak,
⁷let Israel hope for the LORD.
For with the LORD there is mercy,
in him is plentiful redemption.
⁸It is he who will redeem Israel
from all its iniquities.

℣. Eternal rest grant unto them, O Lord.
℟. And let perpetual light shine upon them.

℣. May they rest in peace.
℟. Amen.

Let us pray.

O God, giver of pardon
and loving author of our salvation,
grant, we pray You, in Your mercy, that,
through the intercession of Blessed Mary, ever-Virgin,
and all Your Saints,
the members, friends and
benefactors of our community,
who have passed from this world,
may attain a share in eternal happiness.
Through Christ our Lord. ℟. Amen.

Domina Nostra Publishing

P.O. Box 1464
Monterey, CA. 93942-1464
USA

info@DominaNostraPublishing.com
www.DominaNostraPublishing.com

www.ingramcontent.com/pod-product-compliance
Lightning Source LLC
Chambersburg PA
CBHW062107290426
44110CB00022B/2741